Healing is the
CHILDREN'S BREAD

Taking Authority Over Infirmities

Deneise Fearon

Published by:

DAYELight
PUBLISHERS

ISBN: 978-1-958443-11-8 (paperback)

Unless otherwise stated, Scripture quotations marked KJV are from the Holy Bible, King James Version (Authorized Version). First published in 1611. Quoted from the KJV Classic Reference Bible, Copyright 1983, by The Zondervan Corporation.

Acknowledgment

I must give honour and thanks to my Abba Father in Heaven; thank You for entrusting me with the privilege, gift, and desire to write this book. I am humbled that You have chosen me as one of Your vessels to bless Your people.

To my husband, daughter and siblings, thank you for believing in me; and motivating me through the journey of life and as I wrote this book. I love you, and I am grateful to God for you.

To all my friends, supporters, well-wishers, and prayer warriors, thank you.

To my editor, proofreaders, graphic designers, and all those who helped in making this book a reality; I am grateful for you all. God bless you!

Table of Contents

Foreword

In today's culture, there are many people who don't believe in God's healing power as we would see in the scriptures (even believers). This is a sad because the Word of God tells us God is the same yesterday, today and tomorrow. Since God doesn't change, it means He is able to heal His children from sickness and infirmities as He desires.

The questions many people ask include:

- How do we access His promises of healing?
- Is this healing only available for some people?
- How do we grow our faith to receive healing?

These are a few of the questions minister Deneise Fearon answers in this book *Healing Is the Children's Bread: Taking Authority Over Infirmities.* The author does a great job building the reader's faith to believe God will heal (no matter what disease/sickness they are struggling with). Her personal testimony is also very inspiring and encouraging.

Even if you're not struggling with an illness now, I believe you can also read this book to build your faith on how to pray for others who you know may be sick.

This book is definitely needed for such a time as this.

Crystal S. Daye

Introduction

In September 2020, I was gravely ill. I thought I was coming to the end of my life. The Spirit of the Lord began to minister to me. He reminded me that there is power in my mouth and that I should declare His words of healing over my body. As I opened my mouth and began to speak, the only words I could utter was "Healing is the Children's Bread." I was healed the moment I received those words into my spirit. In the midst of my declaration, the Holy Spirit made it clear that He had given me the title of my third book.

In the content of this book, I share my personal experience of how I was miraculously healed and continue to maintain my healing through faith in God and His Word. I use the scripture as my guide, extracting principles that will encourage and equip you to become intentional about pursuing and maintaining God's divine Healing. I know that some people are desirous of healing but lack faith, as may be the case for you. Hence, I have written *Healing is the Children's Bread: Taking Authority Over Infirmities* to inspire you and challenge your faith to pursue, believe and receive healing from the Lord.

As a child of God, healing belongs to you. Therefore, it is my prayer that as you read this book, you will be convicted and challenged by the Holy Spirit to access what is already yours.

Healing is the Children's Bread

God's words to us are:

But He was wounded for our transgressions, He was bruised for our iniquities, the chastisement of our peace was upon Him and with His stripes, we are healed. (Isaiah 53:5 - KJV).

Chapter One

The Spirit of Infirmity

———•••✳•••———

"… and a woman was there who had been crippled by a spirit for eighteen years. She was bent over and could not straighten up at all. When Jesus saw her, he called her forward and said to her, "Woman, you are set free from your infirmity." Then he put his hands on her, and immediately she straightened up and praised God. Indignant because Jesus had healed on the Sabbath, the synagogue leader said to the people, "There are six days for work. So come and be healed on those days, not on the Sabbath." The Lord answered him, "You hypocrites! Doesn't each of you on the Sabbath untie your ox or donkey from the stall and lead it out to give it water? Then should not this woman, a daughter of Abraham, whom Satan has kept bound for eighteen long years, be set free on the Sabbath day from what bound her?" (St. Luke 13:11-16).

In the story, as recounted in St. Luke 13:11-16, we find a woman who was bent over for eighteen years and who was healed by Jesus on the Sabbath day. You may have thought that the woman could have been taken to any doctor and the problem would be diagnosed, then she would have received some form of medical treatment and the problem would be solved. However, the situation was not a simple medical condition, it was spiritual; one that only God could remedy. The woman had a spirit of infirmity.

The spirit of infirmity describes an unclean spirit that inflicts symptoms of a disease on the host. One who has a spirit of infirmity will find him/herself going through cycles of sickness, temporary relief, then the same sickness manifesting again. Others will be sick for long periods of time with little or no relief. Medication is powerless against this spirit, so it will take spiritual authority to break this spiritual problem. From St. Luke 13, it is clear that evil spirits can sometimes cause physical maladies. Luke's reference to the spirit of infirmity indicates that a demon had been granted the power to inflict a disability. There are some people who refer to the spirit of infirmity as being the cause of sickness, or they may talk about spirits of particular emotions or sins, such as anger or lust.

The church of Jesus Christ is known to have the authority to break this and any other spirit that attacks the mind, body, or spirit. When you understand that authority, you will be bold enough to exercise the power that it gives. Jesus understood His authority, so He was able to speak to the spirit of infirmity. The moment Jesus saw this infirmed woman, He recognized the spirit, called her forward, and dismissed the demon by saying, "Woman, you are set free from your infirmity." He then placed

His hands on her and immediately she straightened up and praised God.

Authority Over Infirmities

One of the greatest needs in the body of Christ is knowing its authority over the world of darkness. Authority is not fabricated mentally. There are rules, protocols, and recognition of true authority. We see this in the story of the sons of Sceva. The demons tore them because they had no true authority (see Acts 19:11-20). The Bible is clear that spiritual warfare exists. Ephesians 6:12 says *"For our struggle is not with flesh and blood, but against the rulers, the authorities against the powers of this dark world and against the spiritual forces of evil in the heavenly realms." (NIV)*.

The authority given to the church is recognized in the realm of the spirit. For greater is He that is in the church, than he that is in the world (see 1 John 4:4). This authority has already been given to us spiritually. We must be able to see it in the spirit and demonstrate it in the physical world. In order to exercise that spiritual authority, we must come to the level of hearing God through faith. Romans 10:17 says faith comes by hearing the message, and the message is heard through the word about Christ.

Sources Of Infirmity

We are apt to think that all bad things come from our common enemy. Sin does tend to be the entrance through which most human afflictions arise. However, there is yet another source. Let us explore both sources.

According to 1st Corinthians 5:5, immorality can be a door to the spirit of infirmity. This means that when one sins, the door opens for the enemy to inflict their bodies with sicknesses and diseases. Such affliction needs more than a doctor's visit. It needs the two antidotes presented in James 5:14-16: repentance and deliverance.

Repentance is relevant and must be done frequently. Our nature is to sin, so sinning is automatic even for a born-again believer, because sometimes we commit the act of sin in our thoughts. That is why the Apostle Paul wrote:

"Finally, brothers and sisters, whatever is true, whatever is noble, whatever is right, whatever is pure, whatever is lovely, whatever is admirable; if anything is excellent or praiseworthy, think about such things." (Philippians 4:8 - NIV).

Not every act of sin requires deliverance but, for example, if you are involved in the act of witchcraft, promiscuity, habitual lying, covetousness, being a drunkard, being prideful, or being an idolator, you will need to go through the process of deliverance.

"Is any sick among you? Let him call for the elders of the church; and let them pray over him, anointing him with oil in the name of the Lord and the prayer of faith shall save the sick, and the

14

Lord shall raise him up; and if he has committed sins, they shall be forgiven him. Confess your faults one to another, and pray one for another, that ye may be healed. The effectual fervent prayer of a righteous man availeth much." (James 5:14-16 - KJV).

In the scripture above, the two antidotes prescribed are the prayers of the elders and confession to another person. These two methods will work if the infirmity was a result of your sin. However, there might be another source of infirmity.

A very powerful question was asked by the disciples *about a man who was blind. His disciples asked him, "Rabbi, who sinned, this man or his parents, that he was born blind?" (John 9:2 - NIV).* In Israel, the widely accepted belief is that the sins of the parents will visit their generations after them, as is stated in Deuteronomy 5:9. This caused the Jews to automatically ascribe any physical deformities or impediments to the sins of the afflicted person's foreparents. However, in *John 9*, Jesus pointed out that this man's affliction was not a result of anyone's sins but rather for the glory of God. As shown in this scripture, the antidote for this was faith.

Prayer is no doubt one of the most significant ingredients in the removal of the spirit of infirmity. You must therefore learn how to pray. Learn to pray according to James 5: 13-14, "*Is any among you afflicted? Let him pray...*"

Chapter Two

My Journey Suffering From Sickle Cell Anaemia

————◆··✳··◆——————

Sickle cell anaemia is a disorder of the blood that causes red blood cells to lose their shape and break down. With sickle cell disease, an inherited group of red blood cells contort into a crescent shape. This leads to the early death of these cells, leaving a shortage of healthy red blood cells which can block blood flow causing pain.

In my childhood years, I was diagnosed with sickle cell anaemia. I can remember that I suffered severely from excruciating joint pain, weakness, nausea, chest pain, headaches, and eye aches as a result of the disease. As I grew older, it became more difficult to live with this disease. It grew more and more unbearable as the years passed. Much of my days were filled with pain and discomfort. Some days I felt like dying was a better option.

There were days that I wasn't able to attend school because of a medical crisis. I was in and out of school for months. I don't like hospitals so one of my worst nightmares was that the hospital had become my place of abode for many months. I was devastated.

My entire family was perturbed by the situation. This disease was like a plague. I can recall a crisis I had one particular night; the pain was so severe.

As I cried out to my late mother to help me, she looked on in anguish and then uttered to me in a very calm tone "Deneise, pray." I had not imagined that I was able to pray because of the intensity of the pain I felt. However, the strength of the Lord was made perfect in my weakness according to 2nd Corinthians 12:9. As I uttered a prayer to the Lord, "Lord, if you heal me, I will serve you for the rest of my life," were the words I spoke to Him. Moments after, I fell asleep and woke up the following day pain free. I was convinced that I had received a touch from the Lord.

A few years passed and the disease was no longer plaguing me. However, as I got older and launched out in my adult years, the reminder came that sickle cell anaemia had not gone anywhere but was still there. The whole ordeal of what I had endured as a child began to resurface during the delivery process of my daughter. Many prayers were made on my behalf, and again, I pulled through. Jesus did it again.

As I continued with life and worked in the corporate setting, sickle cell once more became a plague. There were days when I would be unable to function well on my job, and others when I had to stay home. Though this disease would appear to have had control over my life, there came a time when I had to speak to myself. I came to a place where I understood my authority as a believer and that I needed to exercise it by faith. My desire was that I received healing so I reminded myself of the Word of the Lord in Isaiah 53:5; *"But He was wounded for our transgressions, He was bruised for our iniquities; the chastisement of our peace was upon Him, and by His stripes, we were healed."* (NKJV).

I began to declare it over my body by faith and decided that I would maintain my healing. Today, I still declare it and believe it. I have never had a crisis because of sickle cell anaemia since. God still heals.

Chapter Three

The Second Touch
————•••❋•••————

There is an interesting story recorded in the book of St. Mark 8:22-26 where a blind man was brought to Jesus for healing. After laying His hands on this man, Jesus asked if He could now see. "I see men like trees walking," the man replied. Jesus recognized that healing wasn't complete, He again touched his eyes and his sight was restored, and he saw everything clearly.

The man did not know Jesus. He had a lack of faith and hope that he would be able to see. Lack of faith can be a barrier to receiving your healing. If you are seeking healing, your faith must be built up by the Word of God. The blind man received his first touch from Jesus, and he had a glimpse of the possibility and hope that he was able to receive his sight. What could one touch do for you?

You may have had a similar experience suffering from infirmity. You may have received the first touch, but you are not completely healed and might still be struggling with the ailment. I am reminding you that the Word of the Lord to us is that He desires us to have good health according to *3 John 1:2*. The fact that you have received the first touch and the pain and or struggle is not as severe as before signifies hope and possibility. If you desire healing, you must now begin to take authority and declare the Word of the Lord by faith and you will be healed.

The Lord is waiting for you to request His second touch so that He may release it. If you are struggling to believe that complete healing is possible, also request that He will increase the level of your faith. God understands our inability to exercise the faith we need at times. In Mark 9:24, a man admitted to Jesus that he wanted help with his unbelief. Jesus did not rebuke him. Instead, He healed the man's child. He honoured the man's desire to grow in faith and was pleased that he knew that He, Jesus, was the source of that faith. So, if we have the desire to believe what the Bible teaches, we have the right foundation to continue the fight for faith. God's faithfulness is evident in the Scriptures. His words have been proven to be true over and over again. We have all the evidence we need, but God leaves us to believe. Will you trust Him in this hour as you read and meditate on this chapter? He is willing and ready to touch you again so that you will be healed.

Chapter Four

Ever Increasing Faith

Your faith may need to be stretched for healing. Everyone has been given a measure of faith. This means that we are all born with faith. Since we all have different measures, it means that we all have faith to receive different levels of breakthroughs or miracles. You need to reflect on how you are using your measure of faith to cultivate greater faith. This takes me back to the parable of the talents (see *Matthew 25:14-30*). In that story, we saw that the master required everyone to be industrious with what he was given. You will only experience an increase when you put in the work. That is the rule of productivity.

Faith really grows through hearing the Word of God and the ensuing actions taken. It was James who wrote that faith without works is dead (see *James 2:26*). The Word of God presents the truth and once we apprehend it, we act upon it and that becomes evidence of faith. The more one exercises the measure of faith they have, the more likely it will grow. There were times when I did not have the faith to successfully rebuke a headache, but over time and with the exercising of my faith, I became able to accurately rebuke not only headaches but also more critical pains and illnesses. I found that the more headaches I rebuked, the more confident I became to rebuke the next headache I encountered. What are you doing with your measure of faith?

If we interact with persons of great faith, then we can also begin to operate in great faith. This is so because faith can also be imparted as spoken of by Paul in *1 Timothy 1:5*. In that verse, Paul clearly affirmed that he was certain that the faith which was in Timothy's grandmother and mother must also be in him. *"I am reminded of your sincere faith, which first lived in your grandmother Lois and in your mother Eunice and, I am persuaded, now lives in you also." (NIV)*. This specifically spoke of the clear possibility that faith can be transferred from person to person. Now that you are ready to believe, let us look at the instructions for healing as illustrated in the following chapter.

Chapter Five

Follow Divine Instructions To Receive Divine Healing

————•◦✳◦•————

"I will instruct you and teach you in the way you should go; I will guide you with my eye. Do not be like the horse or like the mule, which have no understanding, which must be harnessed with bit and bridle, Else they will not come near you." (Psalm 32:8-9 - NKJV).

O ur breakthrough is tied to a specific instruction. Divine instructions are imperative for a successful life and are fundamental to one's healing. In the book of 2nd Kings 5:9-13, we read of Naaman, a Syrian general with leprosy who was told that a prophet in Israel named Elisha was able to obtain healing for him. Remember that Naaman was both wealthy and powerful and held a high office in Syria. He went to see the prophet with assigned men, his chariots, and horses. Regardless of Naaman's prestigious status, the prophet Elisha did not come out of his home to greet him. Rather, Elisha gave instructions to a messenger to relay to Naaman what God required him to do to be healed of his leprosy. Naaman was offended because he thought that he deserved more honour. He almost missed out on the opportunity to receive his healing. To make it worse, he was instructed to go dip himself seven times in the muddy Jordan.

The Word of the Lord in 1st Corinthians 1:27 says that "He chooses the foolish things to confound the wise." The Lord is also not a respecter of persons according to Romans 2:11, so it does not matter your status, title, or position in life. That will not dictate the instructions you will receive from God. It is extremely important that whatever instructions you receive are followed exactly.

Are you hesitant about a particular instruction that you have received from the Lord? This instruction might be critical to receiving your healing. There is no good in rejecting God's instructions because that will prevent the healing of the Lord from manifesting. Divine instructions are one way that you can receive healing through faith. Remember, never be hesitant to take action whenever you are given an instruction from the Lord. Naaman followed the instructions given to him by the prophet after he was counseled by his servant. It was only then that he received his complete healing from leprosy (see 2nd Kings 5:9-14).

Hearing The Voice Of God

Naaman received instructions from the Prophet Elisha, but there are other ways you might receive the instructions of God. Let's take a moment to reflect on some of the ways we may hear from God.

God can be heard through His audible voice, scriptures, prayer, the Holy Spirit, church, creation, worship, dreams and visions, impressions, and/or thoughts.

Hearing God's Audible Voice

It is biblical that God speaks audibly. In St. Matthew 17:5, when Jesus was baptised, the Father spoke audibly for others to hear. We see where everyone heard His voice. In this part of the New Testament **"A bright cloud overshadowed them, and a voice from the cloud said, '***This is my beloved son, with whom I am well pleased; listen to Him.'***"** While we understand and can appreciate that God speaks in dreams and visions as well as in a still small voice, the written Word or through prophecy, we understand also that there are times when the audible voice of the Lord is heard.

When Peter visited Joppa, there was a voice that came to him saying, *"Get up, Peter, kill and eat!"* After Peter's response, the voice spoke to him a second and a third time. This happened three times and immediately the object was taken up into the sky (see Acts 10:13-16). This was a physical representation and demonstration of the move of God in a tangible way, where one could hear and see what represented the audible voice of God.

Scriptures

We hear the voice of God through the written Word. This is one of the ways in which God speaks to man. This is also a way in which everyone can hear the voice of God. I truly believe that it is the most effective way in which He speaks to not just some of us but to all of us. There is an answer to every situation that each individual can encounter in the scriptures. If you truly desire to hear God, by reading His Word daily, you are guaranteed to hear Him speak to you.

Deuteronomy 8:3 declares: *"So He humbled you, allowed you to be in hunger, and fed you manna which you did not know nor your fathers did know, that He might make you know that; Man shall not live by bread alone but every word that proceeds out of the mouth of God."*

Prayer

"But without faith it is impossible to please God." But, if as children of God we want to have a relationship with our Father, then prayer should be our daily bread. Prayer is a medium in which we can communicate with the Lord. Through prayer we build a bond and a relationship where the Lord is able to speak to us, correct us and guide us. Whenever we pray, He always listens and then He responds. If you have been praying and not hearing from God, then perhaps you need to take some time to listen. Jeremiah 33:3 declares *"Call unto me and I will answer and I will show you great and mighty things which thou knowest not."*

Holy Spirit

Hearing God through the Holy Spirit is actually hearing God. The Holy Spirit is our guide and leads us into all truth (see John 16:13). The Holy Spirit is not heard through our natural ability but through spiritual discernment. Spiritual discernment is also activated through the reading of the scriptures (see Hebrews 4:12).

Church

The church is the body of Christ. We come together as a body to fellowship and hear from God through the individuals He uses to speak to us in any particular gathering (pastors, worship leaders, prophets, etc.).

Creation

"The heavens declare the glory of God and the firmament sheweth his handy work" (Psalm 19:1 - KJV). As declared in the scriptures, if you should really pause to admire creation and its uniqueness, then you will be able to recognize that they did not create themselves. We have seen the demonstration of God speaking to us through creation by declaring let there be and there was. That was God displaying His beauty and sovereignty through His creation (see Genesis 1).

Worship

To enter into God's presence is to acknowledge who He is and to exalt Him through our worship. When we permeate the atmosphere and release our worship to the Lord, we begin to hear His voice through inner impressions, instructions, and His written Word that is in our hearts. The scripture declares that *"God is a spirit and they that worship Him must worship Him in Spirit and in truth" (St. John 4:24).* When your spirit is connected to the Spirit of the Lord, it permits you to hear Him clearly.

Dreams & Visions

Hearing God through dreams and visions is scriptural. *"And it shall come to pass that afterwards, I will pour out my spirit on all flesh, and your sons and your daughters shall prophesy, your old men shall dream dreams and your young men shall see visions" (Joel 2:28).* I too have personal encounters of hearing God through dreams and visions. It is important to be sensitive to know when God is speaking to you through a dream or a vision. How do you know this? Pray and ask for the spirit of discernment. Discerning the voice of the Lord is critical to hearing Him.

Impression & Thoughts

God speaks through impressions in our thoughts. Have you ever thought about someone you have not seen or heard from in years, then "by chance" encounter them later that day or week, or seen something about them on social media? These impressions often show us how or when to pray for or encourage others.

God also speaks through impressions in our bodies. Sometimes we get a feeling in our body when we are interacting with or praying for someone, and it might correlate with something going on in their body. In these cases, we can simply ask to confirm.

God speaks through impressions in our emotions. This can be a feeling in our soul of what someone else is experiencing, or feeling what the Lord feels for someone to whom we are ministering. Keep in mind that the thoughts God has towards people are always thoughts of love, grace, protection, joy, and conviction; not condemnation or shame (see Jeremiah 29:11).

Accurately discerning God's voice through impressions or thoughts takes discipline, wisdom, trying, and trusting Him.

Chapter Six

Become Desperate For His Touch

ow desperate are you to receive the touch of healing? In the gospel of *St. Luke 8:43-48*, a woman had been suffering from haemorrhaging for twelve years; and though she had spent all she had on physicians, no one could cure her. She came up behind Jesus and touched the fringe of His clothes, and immediately her haemorrhage stopped. Then Jesus asked, who touched me? When all denied it, Peter said, *"Master, the crowd surrounds you and press in on you,"* but Jesus said, *"Someone touched me for I noticed that power had gone out from me."* When the woman saw that she could not remain hidden, she came trembling and fell down before Him, she declared in the presence of all the people why she had touched him, and how she had been immediately healed. Jesus said to her *"Daughter, your faith has made you well, go in peace."* Jesus did with one touch what no doctor could do in twelve years. God is moved to action by our faith, even when He is in the middle of doing something else.

This woman heard the voice of Jesus as He called her into healing, and she was determined not to be enslaved by her physical condition. She was not willing to accept her physical condition and intentionally attempted to be a member of her community again. She had an objective to touch Jesus so that she could be healed. She was desperate. I visualised myself in that woman's position. Can you too?

Knowing that you or a loved one is being hampered by a terminal illness, what do you do in this situation? Would you sit down and continue to endure the pain or give up on the possibility of receiving complete healing? The woman with the issue of blood, as she is popularly called, was at a point in her life where she had to make an important decision. It was do or die for her. She took authority over the situation, stepped out by faith, and pushed through a very thick crowd. Her only hope was to touch Jesus' clothes so she would be healed. That was extraordinary faith in action. She was desperate and knew she had to apply radical faith for her recovery.

The woman pressed both physically and spiritually to receive her healing. What action will you take today concerning yours? Be reminded also that it takes the action of faith to receive healing. The Word of the Lord in Jeremiah 30:17: *"But I will restore you to health and heal your wounds, declares the Lord." (NIV).*

Spiritual Healing

Very often illnesses can have deep-seated spiritual root causes. There might be a spirit, as mentioned before, that is reinforcing infirmity in the host. There are also spiritual wounds that manifest as physical diseases. On the other hand, after being physically ill over a long period of time, there might be negative spiritual effects of these painful physical events. You might have pushed these feelings so far down and as a result, you have not been healed spiritually. These unhealed wounds can cause you to be ineffective in your spiritual life.

Have you been betrayed, rejected, or abused, and the wounds are still open? We can all relate. I have had my share, some of which lasted for a long time. During these times, I did not want to be treated. What does the Bible say about spiritual healing:

"Put away all malice, all deceit and hypocrisy, envy and slander. Like newborn infants long for the pure spiritual milk, that by it you may grow up into salvation if indeed you have tasted that the Lord is good. As you come to Him a living stone rejected by men but in the sight of the Lord, chosen and precious, you yourselves like living stones are being built up as a spiritual house, An holy priesthood, to offer up spiritual sacrifices, acceptable to God by Jesus Christ." (1st Peter 2:1-5 – KJV).

Do you desire to receive healing from betrayal, rejection, abuse, emotional wounds, pains, sorrows, grief, or anguish? Here are some biblical principles that will assist you in receiving spiritual healing:

1. **Release those hurt, painful and fearful emotions into the hands of Jesus.** Holding on to fear, hurt, and pain can block the healing power of the Holy Spirit in your soul. It is vital to open up and allow the Lord to heal your wounds. *Matthew 11:28-30* says *"Come unto me all ye that labour and are heavy laden, and I will give you rest, take my yoke upon you, and learn of me; for I am meek and lowly in heart and ye shall find rest unto your souls, for my yoke is easy and my burden is light." (KJV)*.

   Allow your painful emotions to be released as you give them to the Lord. It is okay to cry and let damaged emotions out as they are given into the hands of the Lord. Holding onto the pain and hurt will only prevent you from being healed. Remember that you are sustained by your spirit. So your spirit must be free and your emotions clear of clutter.

2. **Realize the love of God for you.** Knowing the true nature of our Heavenly Father will help us to trust Him and open ourselves up so we can receive the healing that only the Holy Spirit can provide for us. You are loved by God, not because of who you are but because of who He is.

   "But *God commendeth His love towards us, in that while we were yet sinners; Christ died for us. Jesus said the greatest love a man can show for his friends is when he lays down his life for them. Jesus laid down His life for*

us, that is how valuable and dear we are to Him."
(Romans 5:8 – NIV).

3. **Realize God's will for your mind and receive it.** Romans
   12:2 says, *"And be not conformed to this world: but be*
   ye transformed by the renewing of your mind, that ye
   may prove what is that good, acceptable and perfect will
   of God." (KJV). Are you considering what the mind has
   to do with an emotional wound? I want to inform you
   that when you are wounded by your emotions, your mind
   and willpower are weakened under the pressure. The
   scriptures call this a broken spirit. This will literally make
   you sick. *"A cheerful heart is good medicine, but a*
   crushed spirit dries up the bones." (Proverbs 17:22 –
   NIV).

The flesh will want us to become consumed by self-pity.
However, when we focus on our own pains, we open ourselves
up to the enemy because we are dwelling on the hurt instead of
believing in the healing. We can come against the enemy by
focusing on God and what He would have us do. In doing all of
that, we open ourselves to receive divine healing from the
Almighty God.

Chapter Seven

Make A Covenant With God By Faith

——•••✳•••——

Deuteronomy 7:9 "Know therefore that the Lord your God is God, the faithful God which keeps covenant and mercy with them that love Him and keep His commandments to a thousand generations." (KJV).

Exodus 23:25 "And ye shall serve the Lord your God, and He shall bless thy bread, and thy water; and I will take sickness away from the midst of thee." (KJV).

G od is a covenant keeper according to His Word, so He requires us to be covenant keepers as well. If you desire healing, then entering a covenant is a powerful way in which you may receive the same. Our covenant with God includes healing.

Many times over, we hear stories of persons having near-death experiences and evoking a covenant with God for the length of days. It usually includes the person promising to serve the Lord all the days of his or her life in exchange for healing or deliverance. A similar covenant was initiated by Jonah, who, after he had tried to evade the purpose of the Lord, found himself in the belly of a whale. He cried out to the Lord and went into a covenant with Him in exchange for his deliverance. The whale delivered Jonah to the shore of his purpose, and the rest is history (see Jonah 2:1-10).

God has entered an everlasting covenant that provides for all our needs, including healing, and He has bound Himself to us with His Word. According to Psalm 89:34, He promised "My covenant will I not break, nor alter the thing that is gone out of my lips." (KJV). From His very first dealings with the children of Israel, God's purpose was to remove sickness from among His people. He entered into a covenant of healing with them in the wilderness. He told them, according to Exodus 15:26:

"If thou wilt diligently hearken to the voice of the Lord thy God and wilt do that which is right in His sight, and will give ear to His commandments, and keep all His statues, I will put none of these diseases upon thee, which I have brought upon the Egyptians: for I am the Lord that healeth thee." (KJV).

God wanted His people to know that not only was He their mighty deliverer, but He was also their Jehovah Rapha, the God who heals them. On Mount Sinai, after He gave the ten commandments, He promised that He would take away sicknesses from the midst of them (see Exodus 23:25). Forty years later, as they prepared to enter the promised land, Moses reminded them of the covenant and God's promise for healing.

"*Wherefore it shall come to pass, if ye hearken to these judgments, keep and do them, that the Lord thy God shall keep unto thee the covenant and the mercy which He sware unto thy fathers; thou shalt be blessed above all people; there shall not be male or female barren among you, or your cattle. And the Lord will take away from her all sickness and will put none of the evil diseases of Egypt, which thou knowest, upon thee; but will lay them upon all them that hate thee.*" *(Deuteronomy 7:12-15 - KJV).*

God has planned for His people to be free from illnesses and diseases and to live in divine health. When the children of Israel entered the promised land, there was not one feeble among them. "*He brought them forth also with silver and gold; and there was not one feeble person among their tribe.*" *(Psalm 105:37 - KJV).* In the same way that the Lord entered into a covenant with Israel, which included their healing and the removal of sickness from among them, He has entered a covenant with you that provides for your healing. All you have to do is believe.

Faith is one very important tool that you can use to come into covenant with God. Find the details of the covenant, make the declaration by faith, and you will experience the healing of Jehovah Rapha.

Declaration: Abba, Jehovah Rapha, thank You for Your covenant, which includes healing for me. I acknowledge that I am

in covenant with You, and I declare that today is my day to receive all of the promises You have for me, in Jesus Christ's name. Amen!

Chapter Eight

A Covenant Keeping God

My covenant will I not break, nor alter the thing that is gone out of my lips. (Psalm 89:34 - KJV).

There is nothing more comforting than entering into an agreement with someone who we know will honour their part. In a covenant with God, there are some very powerful words that we must remember.

God is not a man that he should lie (see Numbers 23:19 - KJV).

The Lord is not slack concerning His promise
(see 2nd Peter 3:9 - KJV).

He keeps covenants to a thousand generations (see
Deuteronomy 7:9 - NIV).

His word is yea and yea and amen
(see 2nd Corinthians 1:20 - KJV).

His word shall not return to Him void
(see Isaiah 55:11 - KJV).

Healing is the Children's Bread

When God entered into a covenant with Abram, He told him that he would be the father of many nations. Abram did not live to see this word fulfilled but God was careful to honour His Word. Whether you are dead or alive, whatever God has promised concerning your descendant will happen. God has sworn by Himself and He cannot break His own Word.

Covenants show God's true and loyal nature. If He says He will do something, He will not break that promise. In the Bible promises meant life or death, unlike today.

We can also see God's faithful fulfillment of other covenants, even when humans sinned and did not hold up their end. Praise the Lord that we have such a wonderful God who fulfills His covenants and promises.

God is willing and ready to manifest His covenant of healing in your life and body. BE HEALED TODAY!

Chapter Nine

Being Intentional About Your Covenant

I n order for you to become intentional about a covenant, you must understand what a covenant is. A covenant is an agreement between God and His people, in which God makes promises to His people and usually requires a certain conduct from them.

There are a number of significant covenants in the Bible, such as the Mosaic covenant that God made with Israel. The Lord told Moses in Exodus 19 that if Israel upheld the condition to faithfully listen and obey, God would uphold His end of the covenant. In other words, the Israelites were to become guardians of God's covenant. That meant living out the commandments as a light to the nations.

"Now, therefore, if you will indeed obey my voice and keep my covenant, you shall be my treasured possession among all peoples, for all the earth is mine." (Exodus 19:5).

Unique Calling

The basis for the calling of Israel was to be a priest for the nations of the earth. God called Israel in the midst of a people who walked in darkness. They were people who did not live according to any laws, but God chose the nation of Israel to set forth His example on the earth.

God destined the Jewish people to bring forth His Messiah. He would bring redemption to all the nations of the earth. Living out the commandments meant that Israel was to recognise its calling. It made them God's people, His own special possession.

"Know therefore that the Lord your God is God, the faithful God who keeps covenant and steadfast love with those who love him and keep his commandments, to a thousand generations." (Deuteronomy 7:9 - ESV).

Because a Covenant includes two or more parties who each have a responsibility in that covenant, breaking a covenant usually attracts a penalty. You can rest assured that God will not be the one to break a covenant.

In Genesis 12:1-3, the Lord said to Abram, *"go from your country, your people and your father's household to the land that I will show you. I will make you into a great nation and I will bless you; I will make your name great and you will be a blessing.*

I will bless those who bless you and I will curse those who curse you and all people on earth will be blessed through you."

In the text, the Lord made a covenant with Abram and promised a great reward. Abram was careful to note the promises of God over his life so he was intentional about following the instructions that were given to him by the Lord. He was willing to act accordingly. Abram was very obedient in that even though he was unaware of where the Lord was sending him, he was willing to go. The act of faith established the covenant. Abram was willing to do His part, so the God of covenants would do His part to a thousand generations.

When you make a covenant with God for your healing, you must be intentional about it. Being intentional about obedience and faith are major ingredients. How long have you been praying for healing and deliverance but you have been neither consistent nor insistent about it? Whenever you ask the Lord for anything, you must be careful to follow through with the instructions that you receive.

I remember while struggling with sickle cell anaemia, I made a covenant with the Lord telling Him that I would serve Him for the rest of my life if He healed me. I was determined to receive and maintain my healing so I sealed my covenant by taking the necessary steps to ensure that my covenant was kept. I will admit that it was not easy. I had struggles but I was determined to maintain healing. How is your faith, obedience, and willpower concerning your covenant? At this point, you may need to do an introspection to see whether or not you are being intentional. As you make the adjustments, you shall receive your breakthrough.

Chapter Ten

Going The Extra Mile

————•◆•❋•◆•————

If you desire something, then it is a requirement, more often than not, to go the extra mile in order to achieve it. Thus, we move on from being intentional to moving by faith into that extra mile.

St. Luke 5:17-20 says: "One day, while Jesus was teaching, some proud religious law keepers and teachers of the law were sitting by Him. They had come from every town in the countries of Galilee and Judea and from Jerusalem. The power of the Lord was there to heal them. Some men took a man who was not able to move his body to Jesus. They looked for a way, but they could not find a way to take the man into the house where Jesus was, because of the crowd. They made a hole in the roof over where Jesus stood. Then they let down the bed with the sick man in the midst of where Jesus was. When Jesus saw their faith, He said to the man, friend your sins are forgiven."

In this story, we see where going the extra mile is demonstrated. As I reflected on the story, it stood out to me that these men became desperate for the healing of their friend. As a result of their desperation, they were determined to do whatever it took for their friend to receive his healing. They were both desperate and intentional, and it paid off.

How desperate are you to receive your healing? If you are truly tired of the pain, then you must be willing to take drastic actions. Some of these actions may include getting rid of the toxins in your life through deeper relationships with the Lord. Toxins such as malice, jealousy, hatred, pride, lust, lying, and covetousness just to name a few. Harbouring these spirits will result in being spiritually malnourished. We can never ignore the power of fasting, prayer, and worship in the healing process.

Fasting

This is a powerful way to come into your healing and deliverance. Fasting is making the sacrifice, turning down those pots and plates as the need arises to focus on a particular goal. It is an act of sacrifice that demonstrates what you are willing to give for what you need. Of course, there are different types of fastings. People fast from things or experiences which otherwise would distract them, but a food fast that afflicts the soul and opens up a true spiritual hunger for God will attract His nearness. *"Draw near to God and He will draw near to you."* (James 4:8 - ESV). What better way to draw close to the Lord than through fasting with prayer?

There was a situation in which a boy was vexed with a devil. The disciples tried to cast it out but were unsuccessful. When the boy was brought to Jesus, the deliverance happened immediately. The disciples were curious about why they were unable to do the deliverance themselves. The answer Jesus gave was the tell tale.

"This kind can come out by nothing but prayer and fasting." (*Mark 9:29 - KJV*).

Fasting awakens the faith and spiritual alertness of the believer to the things of the Spirit. Fasting has a way of making mountains seem like smooth plains by giving the believer the awakened awareness of His authority. You might need to fast.

Prayer

To pray is to come into fellowship with God. It is an intimate exchange between heaven and earth. To pray is to meet with the Almighty God to reason, petition, or pour out your request. There was a lesson taught in the New Testament by way of a parable to express the power of prayer. *".....men ought always to pray, and not to faint." (St. Luke 18:1 - KJV).* Earlier we spoke about hearing God's voice. Prayer is one of those methods that positions you to hear from God. In St. Luke 18, Jesus went on to teach that constant prayer will move the heart of even an unjust judge. How much more will it move the heart of our living Father God.

As you press in for healing, it is very important to commune with the Lord in order to hear His instructions concerning your condition.

Worship

There is another important ingredient in your process of seeking the Lord. As you fast and pray, you should express adoration unto the Lord. Through worship, you can show gratitude for what you have and will receive. Worship has a way of catapulting us into the presence of the Lord where we can experience the fullness of joy and His rhema Word. Be consistent in your worship and let it flow from your heart. Play some music, shut away with God, and flow. You should also consider making worship your continuous attitude. Have a posture of worship. Do not murmur or complain, rather, choose the attitude of gratitude.

Chapter Eleven

The Power Of Declaration
⸰•❈•⸰

*P*roverbs 18:21 puts it this way - *"the tongue has the power of life and death."* The stakes are high; your words can either bring life or death. Our tongue can build others up, or they can tear them down. An unchecked fire doubles in size every minute. Gossip and false teachings are no different. However, words can also bring healing and deliverance.

Jesus entered the world for a single purpose; to destroy the works of the devil (see *1st John 3:8*). As evident in scriptures, two of the main consequences of Satan's influence on the world are sicknesses and diseases. We have been chosen to make all things new; healing was front and center and was consistently modeled by His followers. Healing remained a crucial ministry of the Holy Spirit even after Jesus' ascension.

The disciples of Jesus Christ's earthly ministry were intentional about healing and its administration. They never asked if it was God's will to heal. Instead, because they knew God's will for healing according to the scriptures and their observation of Jesus, they declared healing upon those who needed it. The same authority is given to you. You may have been struggling with a particular sickness or disease, and you may have been reluctant to declare healing by faith. As you read this chapter, pause for a moment and take the time to declare healing in your body in Jesus' name. It will be done to you according to the measure of your faith.

Declaration: I command you sickness (call its name) to leave my body with your cause and symptoms. By the stripes of Jesus Christ, I was healed. I break your hold off my life, in Jesus' mighty name! Amen.

2nd Kings 4:8-37 recounts a story of a wealthy woman from Shunem who took great care of the prophet Elisha. In response to her kindness, Elisha offered to do something special for her. When she refused, Gehazi, Elisha's servant, suggested that the childless woman might appreciate the promise of a son. Despite her protest and fear of disappointment, Elisha made the declaration. Just as the prophet of God had said, the woman conceived and bore a son.

Several years later, the child of the prophet's declaration mysteriously died. His mother's decisive action and determined response drew the attention of the prophet. She was determined, and the man of God was willing to make another declaration. Suffice to say, the dead boy was brought back to life. This miracle was wrapped up in both the mother's declaration that all was well and the prophet's decisive actions.

The power of declaration is a wonderful truth. We see it all over scriptures. The prophets and apostles made powerful statements that stood the test of time and changed people's lives. Therefore, may God inspire the words you speak, for the power of life and death is in the tongue.

To aid you in declaring God's healing over your life, here are a few selected scriptures that you may use:

Psalm 103:2-3: Bless the Lord, O my soul and forget not all his benefits, who forgiveth all thine iniquities who healeth all thy diseases.

Isaiah 53:5: But He was wounded for our transgressions, He was bruised for our iniquities; the chastisement of our peace was upon Him and with His stripes we are healed.

Matthew 4:23: And Jesus went throughout all Galilee, teaching in their synagogues, and preaching the gospel of the kingdom, and healing all manner of disease among the people.

Romans 8:11: If the spirit of Him who raised Jesus from the dead dwells in you, He who raised Christ Jesus from the dead will also give life to your mortal bodies through His spirit who dwells in you.

Healing is the Children's Bread

Psalm 41:3: The Lord supports; (He will sustain, refresh and strengthen) me on my sick bed; He completely heals me from my illness.

Jeremiah 30:17: But I will restore you to health and heal your wounds; declares the Lord.
Isaiah 54:17: No weapon (sickness is a weapon of the enemy) formed against me shall prosper, this is my heritage as a servant of the Lord.

Proverbs 4:20-22: I give attention to God's words; I incline my ear to His sayings. I do not let them depart from my eyes; I keep them in the midst of my heart; for they are life and health to all my flesh.

1st John 5:14-15: Now this is the confidence that I have in Him, that if I ask anything according to His will, he hears me (sickness is not His will). And if I know that He hears me, whatever I ask, I know that I have the petitions that I have asked of Him.

Declare it!

Because God's Spirit lives in me, He gives me life and strength. He brings healing to my body. I am healed, in Jesus' name. Amen.

Chapter Twelve

Unusual Occurrence

According to the gospel of Mark, a man who was deaf and dumb was brought to Jesus. He was the focus of this historical account. Someone cared for this man enough to share with him that the miracle worker was passing by (see *Mark 7:32*). It would have been impossible for him to know that Jesus was in the region of Sidon or even to be sitting on the hill unless someone informed him. Someone had compassion for the man and brought him to Jesus and begged Him to heal him. How did Jesus respond? Jesus took him aside from the crowd and put his fingers into his ears, and after spitting, He touched his tongue with the saliva and looked up to heaven with a deep sigh, *He said to him "Ephphatha!"' That is "be opened"* (St. Mark 7:33-34). The declaration was good enough, and the miraculous happened!

Some people would not have agreed with that demonstration. This action would be classified as unsanitary. However, in the story, we saw where submission had been displayed. You must come to a place of total surrender and also act in obedience to the instructions from the Lord in order to receive your healing.

Healing is the Children's Bread

There was another situation where the instructions were quite unusual. In the story of *1 Kings 17: 1-4*, the Prophet Elijah found himself in a famine, which was the result of a drought he had declared. He needed provision so that he would not die of hunger. A strange instruction came.

'Now Elijah the Tishbite, who was among the settlers of Gilead, said to Ahab, "As surely as the LORD lives—the God of Israel before whom I stand—there will be neither dew nor rain in these years except at my word!" Then a revelation from the LORD came to Elijah: "Leave here, turn eastward, and hide yourself by the Brook of Cherith, east of the Jordan. And you are to drink from the brook, and I have commanded the ravens to feed you there."' (NIV).

Though this account with Elijah had nothing to do with healing, he showed the power of obedience in accessing the promises of God. Are you desperate for healing but reluctant to carry out strange instructions? You might be standing in the way of your own miracle.

Let us take a look at another strange occurrence. There was a man who was sitting at the temple gate, and who was described as being lame from his mother's womb. He came into contact with Peter and John, and through his obedience to a strange instruction, he received a miracle.

Acts 3:1-10 - "*Now Peter and John went up together into the temple at the hour of prayer, being the ninth hour. And a certain man lame from his mother's womb was carried, whom they laid daily at the gate of the temple which is called Beautiful, to ask alms of them that entered into the temple; Who seeing Peter and John about to go into the temple asked an alms. And Peter, fastening his eyes upon him with John, said, Look on us. And he gave heed unto them, expecting to receive something of them. Then Peter said, Silver and gold have I none; but such as I have give I thee: In the name of Jesus Christ of Nazareth rise up and walk. And he took him by the right hand, and lifted him up: and immediately his feet and ankle bones received strength. And he leaping up stood, and walked, and entered with them into the temple, walking, and leaping, and praising God.*" (KJV).

The instructions given to this lame man would have been seen as very strange. How could one ask a lame person to rise up and walk? However, the man's willingness and obedience, with the assistance of Peter, were enough to heal him completely. Will thou be made whole?

Jehovah Rapha is still in the healing business. His miracles are available to you. Have you missed or acted in disobedience to a critical instruction? You can ask the Lord what He would have you do. When He speaks, do not hesitate. Just do it! At this moment, if you come to that place of divine instruction, though it might be strange, nothing will prevent the healing power of

Jesus from manifesting in you. All things are possible to him that believes (see Mark 9:23).

Chapter Thirteen

Faith To Receive The Healing Virtue

————◆◆✳◆◆————

Accordingto the Merriam-Webster dictionary: "healing is to make free from injury or disease; to make sound or whole." To make well again: to restore to health. Christians should approach healing in a biblical way, and in scripture we discover the source and purposes for healing, as well as instructions and models for asking in faith.

Healing comes from God. There is no scripture that condemns the legitimate use of doctors, but one of the names of God is Jehovah Rapha, meaning "the Lord who heals." Healing also comes through the agency of the Holy Spirit working through believers' spiritual gifts (see Acts 3: 1-13).

Jesus healed every disease and sickness among the people in Galilee, Judea, and everywhere that He went. In doing this, He authenticated His Messiahship and gave Israel a taste of the kingdom.

Matthew 4:23 – "*Jesus went throughout Galilee, teaching in their synagogues, proclaiming the good news of the kingdom, and healing every disease and sickness among the people.*"

Matthew 19:1-2 – "*When Jesus had finished saying these things, he left Galilee and went into the region of Judea to the other side of the Jordan. Large crowds followed him, and he healed them there.*"

Mark 6:56 – "*And wherever he went—into villages, towns or countryside—they placed the sick in the marketplaces. They begged him to let them touch even the edge of his cloak, and all who touched it were healed.*" *(NIV).*

John 7:31 – "*Still, many in the crowd believed in him. They said, "When the Messiah comes, will he perform more signs than this man?""* *(NIV).*

Luke 11:20 – "*But if I drive out demons by the finger of God, then the kingdom of God has come upon you.*" *(NIV).*

Only believe

You may hinder healing through the lack of faith. According to Matthew 9:20-22, a lack of faith can hinder what God wants to do. He is more inclined to respond to prayers of faith in powerful, sometimes unexpected ways, as rehearsed about Elijah in James 5:17-18. Going to God with timid prayers may also hinder healing. You will need to pray with confidence, trusting God's goodness and grace (see Matthew 7:11). Pray with conviction that God will reward those who diligently seek Him (see Hebrews 11:6).

Failing to surrender to God's purposes may hinder healing. Humility and readiness to receive what God has for you will help to cooperate with the Word of God. Romans 8:28-29 says, "*And we know that in all things God works for the good of those who love him, who have been called according to his purpose. For those God foreknew he also predestined to be conformed to the image of his Son, that he might be the firstborn among many brothers and sisters.*" *(NIV).*

As you pray for healing, you must believe that all things are working together for your good and that God wants you healed. You must intentionally surrender your will to receive healing; even Jesus surrendered His will in prayer. Luke 22:42 says, "*Father, if you are willing, take this cup from me; yet not my will, but yours be done.*"

Do you possess enough faith to receive your healing today? Do you believe the words of the Lord? Psalm 147:3 declares, "*He healeth the broken in heart, and bindeth up their wounds.*" Since He heals all wounds, that is, mental, emotional, and spiritual; how much more physical wounds?

Healing is the Children's Bread

Luke 1:37 declares, *"for with God nothing shall be impossible."* Also, Jeremiah 30:17 declares *"for I will heal thee of thy wounds saith the Lord."* Accessing faith through the Word of God is the main ingredient to receiving the healing you desire.

Ask For Healing

Did you request healing? You may neglect healing by failing to ask for it.

"You desire but do not have, so you kill. You covet but you cannot get what you want, so you quarrel and fight. You do not have because you do not ask God. Have you asked?" (James 4:2).

According to John 5:6-7, Jesus asked the lame man if he wanted to get well. It might seem strange to ask a man who had been lame for thirty-eight years such a question. It could be that Jesus saw that he was reluctant because he was addicted to the attention and charity he received from being ill. Perhaps his lameness became entwined with his identity. The Lord wants to heal you but have you bothered to ask Him?

"Ask and it will be given to you; seek and you will find; knock and the door will be opened to you. For everyone who asks receives; the one who seeks finds; and to the one who knocks, the door will be opened." (Matthew 7:7-8 - NIV).

Unconfessed Sins

Unconfessed sin may hinder healing. Remember the admonition in James 5:16 to confess our sins to each other and pray for each other so that we may be healed. Confession is important in preparation for healing.

"But your iniquities have separated between you and your God, and your sins have hid his face from you, that he will not hear." (Isaiah 59:2 - *KJV*).

As you prepare for your healing, you must get rid of unconfessed sins. After all, God says He is hindered by our sins. Examine yourself, repent, and prepare the grounds for God to move in your life.

Chapter Fourteen

Jehovah Rapha

———•◦•❖•◦•———

The meaning of the name Jehovah Rapha can be traced back to two Hebrew words, which in combination can mean "God who heals." Jehovah, which is derived from the Hebrew word Havah, can be translated as "to be," "to exist" or "to become known." The Hebraic translation of Rapha means "to restore" or "to heal." Jehovah Rapha is also recognised as Yahweh Rapha.

The varying manifestations of God's tremendous healing power as Jehovah Rapha can be found in the following biblical passages to combat particular ailments:

Sickness and fatigue: *"He restores my soul; He leads me in the paths of righteousness for His name's sake."* (Psalms 23:3).

Emotional suffering: *"For the enemy has persecuted my soul; he has crushed my life down to the ground; he has made me to dwell in darkness, as those who have been long dead."* (Psalms 147:3).

Anxiety and worry: "*Peace I leave with you. My peace I give unto you. Not as the world gives do I give to you. Let not your heart be troubled, neither let it be afraid.*" (John 14:27).

You must understand that our God, named Jehovah Rapha, the healer, is able to heal you of anything for which you may need healing. Perhaps you are struggling with emotional, physical, relational, and mental pain; He can heal you today.

God is the one who heals. While He was on earth, through Jesus, there were more than seventy recorded instances of healing throughout the gospels. Jesus repeatedly said, "be made whole." Wholeness is God's ultimate desire for us.

We all need physical, emotional, moral, or relationship healing at various times in our lives. In whatever area you may require healing, God can do it. I challenge you to listen to the voice of the Lord through scriptures and communicate with Him through prayer. Seek Godly counsel through His servants and put your confidence and faith in Him. God Almighty wants to be your Jehovah Rapha.

Chapter Fifteen

Guard Your Temple

———•·•❋•·•———

"Gracious words are like a honeycomb, sweetness to the soul and health to the body." (Proverbs 16:24).

When it comes to your healing, there is a spiritual aspect as well as a practical application. The Lord has gifted your body with the remarkable ability to heal itself under the right conditions. You need to feed it wholesome food, drink clean water and breathe pure air. It is unfortunate that finding these things is very difficult in our fallen world, as toxic chemicals have overtaken our soil, water, and atmosphere. Despite our many efforts to purchase essential products for a healthy home, we still get sick. Thank God, who has provided His divine healing.

The healing touch of Jesus is powerful and effective. Once God does His part, we must do our part. He heals us, and we maintain the healing. Exodus 23:25 declares *"worship to the Lord your God and His blessing will be on your food and water. I will take away sickness from among you."* We are spirit beings, clothed with our physical bodies. The Bible teaches this according to

Thessalonians 5:23 that we consist of body, soul, and spirit. Therefore, our spirits need a body to reside in. As a result, we must use the principles and the Word of the Lord coupled with us taking care of our bodies to ensure that our temples are protected from sickness and diseases.

God expects us to be good stewards of the physical body He gave us. Since we will only have one body to endure this life, it only makes sense that we take good care of it.

Sometimes while we travel, we will see homes and other things that are abandoned because no one lives there anymore; therefore, no attention is being given to the property. The property then deteriorates until someone else comes and looks after it. The same thing will happen to the body if it is not properly fed and taken care of. This should not be your reality. You must not neglect, abuse, or destroy the body that the Lord has given you. There should be no shortchanging when it comes to taking care of your body.

1st Corinthians 6:19 declares, *"What? Know ye not that your body is the temple of the Holy Ghost which is in you, which ye have of God, and ye are not your own? For we are bought with a price: therefore glorify God in your body and in your spirit, which are God's."* Considering that God has made it abundantly clear that our bodies and spirits are His property, we need to follow His instructions on how to take care of them. We must cater to the physical temple, even as we cater to the spiritual man.

70

God's will is that we are healthy, blessed, and have the peace of the Holy Spirit at work in our lives. Worry, pain and sickness will become a thing of the past once we take care of the physical body, the spiritual man, and put our confidence and trust in the spoken word of Jesus Christ over our temple.

Chapter Sixteen

The Promise

———◆··◆✦◆··◆———

M any times we tend to question the promises of God concerning us, especially when things seem to not be going in the way that we desire them to go. It is with great assurance that I remind you that God's promises are intentional and true. Matthew 23:35 tells us that heaven and earth will pass away, but the Word of God will not. Though this passage of scripture could be in the context of end-time prophecies, I believe it can also be interpreted in the context of God's promises to us.

Though we live each day with the expectancy and grief of sickness and death, that was not God's original plan. But because of sin, we are now faced with the consequences of man's disobedience. However, that is not all, "*God is plenteous in mercy unto all them that call upon Him.*" (Psalm 86:5), "*and He watches over His words to perform it.*" (Jeremiah 1:12). He is still faithful. His promises still stand, and healing is one of them.

God's Promises To Us

Beloved, I pray that you may prosper in all things and be in health, just as your soul prospers." (3 John 1:2).

"Jesus went about all the cities and villages, teaching in their synagogues, preaching the gospel of the kingdom, and healing every sickness and every disease among the people." (Matthew 9:35).

"The whole multitude sought to touch Him, for power went out from Him and healed them all." (Luke 6:19).

"Jesus Christ is the same yesterday, today, and forever." (Hebrews 13:8).

"Bless the LORD, O my soul, and forget not all His benefits: who forgives all your iniquities, who heals all your diseases." (Psalm 103:2-3).

"He was wounded for our transgressions, He was bruised for our iniquities; the chastisement for our peace was upon Him, and by His stripes we are healed." (Isaiah 53:5).

"Heal me, O LORD, and I shall be healed; save me, and I shall be saved, for You are my praise." (Jeremiah 17:14).

"If you diligently heed the voice of the LORD your God and do what is right in His sight, give ear to His commandments and

keep all His statutes, I will put none of the diseases on you which I have brought on the Egyptians. For I am the LORD who heals you." (Exodus 15:26).

"My son, give attention to my words; incline your ear to my sayings. Do not let them depart from your eyes; keep them in the midst of your heart; for they are life to those who find them, and health to all their flesh." (Proverbs 4:20-22).

"He sent His word and healed them, and delivered them from their destruction." (Psalm 107:20).

"Is anyone among you sick? Let him call for the elders of the church, and let them pray over him, anointing him with oil in the name of the Lord. And the prayer of faith will save the sick, and the Lord will raise him up. And if he has committed sins, he will be forgiven." (James 5:14-15).

"These signs will follow those who believe... They will lay hands on the sick, and they will recover." (Mark 16:17-18).

Chapter Seventeen

How To Maintain Your Healing

It is very critical to understand how to receive healing and maintain it. Understanding God's Word and acting on it brings healing to our body, soul, and spirit. Jesus Christ came so that we can have life and have it more abundantly. He came to destroy the works of the devil (see 1 John 3:8). Sickness is one of the results of the oppression of the devil.

The devil inflicts us with sickness and does not like it when God's Word brings healing and destroy his works. The devil will always try to reestablish his infliction by trying to steal the truth of the Word from us. We see this in Matthew 13:19: *"When anyone hears the word of the Kingdom and does not understand it, the evil one comes and snatches away what has been sown in his heart."*

This is a reflection on the one whose seed was sown beside the road. The enemy wants to steal the Word before it can become firmly rooted in us to produce healing. He knows that the Word of God is more powerful than his work of sickness. Therefore, he will try to cut off the word in us before it gets to a place where it can grow and bring forth fruit.

Only seeds that are firmly rooted will produce a harvest. Coming into the harvest of healing is God's desire for us according to His divine Word. Matthew 13:21 says, "*because of the Word, this affliction will be brought against us once again to cause us to fall away.*" Our faith in Jesus and the healing He gave will be challenged and tested. The devil will once again bring the symptoms of the sickness to convince us that we are not healed.

If he can cause us to be focused on symptoms instead of God and His promises, he can convince us to believe his lie. When the focus is on symptoms and pain, then doubt and unbelief come to our mind, and this allows fear to re-establish the sickness.

Keys To Maintaining Your Healing

Faith

Faith comes by hearing and hearing by the Word of God. Faith is believing what God says in His Word regardless of our opinions. When you take the Word of God in your heart and declare it out of your mouth, it becomes God's Word applied to the problem. If you will keep your declaration in line with the Word of God, then sustained healing is inevitable.

Prayer, Praise, and Worship

It is imperative to offer prayer, praise, and worship when you receive healing. This is how you execute the triumph of Jesus Christ over the powers of darkness; Jesus has defeated sin, sickness, disease, death, and poverty and made us free. *"He has redeemed us from the curse of the law."* (Galatians 3:13-14). It has already been accomplished as written in the Word of God.

Meditate On And Live By The Word Of God

Meditation on God's Word brings revelation, and revelation brings the manifestation of healing. *"For they are life to those who find them"* (Proverbs 4:22). Keeping the Word in the midst of our hearts will bring health to our flesh. *"Give attention to my words; incline your ear to my sayings, keep them in the midst of your heart."* Even after receiving healing, the Word of God must be our daily bread.

Chapter Eighteen

Neglect Negative Utterances

------◆•◆✖◆•◆------

It is true that negative utterances can cause serious implications if we are consumed by them. There is a story in the book of St. John chapter 5:1-15 about a man who was healed at the pool of Bethesda. In this story, there is an account of a feast of the Jews which was held in Jerusalem. Being a Jew, Jesus would partake in this feast, so He went up to Jerusalem. Now there is in Jerusalem by the Sheep Gate a pool, which is called in Hebrew, Bethesda, having five porches. In these lay a great multitude of sick people, blind, lame, paralyzed, waiting for the move of the water.

An angel went down at a certain time into the pool and stirred up the water; then, whoever stepped in first, after the stirring of the water, was made well of whatever disease he had. Now a certain man was there who had a spirit of infirmity for thirty-eight years and when Jesus saw him lying there and knew that he had already been in that condition a long time, He said to him *"Do you want to be made well?"*

The sick man answered Him "Sir, I have no man to put me into the pool when the water is stirred up; but while I am coming, another steps down before me."

Jesus said to him, "*Rise, take up your bed and walk.*" Immediately the man was made well, took up his bed, and walked. That was the Sabbath; the Jews therefore said to him who was cured, "*It is the Sabbath; is it not unlawful for you to carry your bed?*" He answered them, "*He who made me well said to me, 'take up your bed and walk!'*"

Then they asked him, "*Who is the Man who said to you, take up your bed and walk?*" But the one who was healed didn't know who it was, for Jesus had withdrawn, a multitude being in that place. Afterward Jesus found him in the temple and said to him, "See you have been made well. Sin no more, lest a worse thing come upon you." The man departed and told the Jews that it was Jesus who had healed him.

According to the story, amazingly, not everyone was happy about the man's miraculous healing. They were more concerned about which day it was so they began to ask negative questions and made statements that they thought would justify the action of the man being healed on the Sabbath day.

In the process of receiving healing, breakthroughs, or deliverance, there are some people that the enemy will use to distract you from receiving it or even cause you to doubt the miraculous manifestations of Jesus Christ in your situation. Had the man internalised their negative questions and comments, he would probably have doubted the healing that he had received and would not have been able to maintain it. Even as they tried to intimidate him with their words, according to the command of Jesus, he received his healing and went his way and sinned no more. As you too receive divine healing from Jesus, it is imperative that you neglect negative utterances.

Chapter Nineteen

The Sent Word

"He sends forth His word and heals them and rescues them from the pit and destruction." (Psalm 107:20).

The written Word of Jesus, when applied, brings forth the manifestation of healing and deliverance. The Word of the Lord is key to every and any situation that we are faced with.

In the book of Acts, there was a man named Aeneas who had been paralysed for eight years. This man obviously heard of Jesus and the account of how He had brought healing and deliverance to the people wherever He went. It is seen in Acts 8:34, where Simon said to Aeneas, "*Jesus Christ heals you. Rise up and smooth out your pallet. And immediately he rose up.*" Aeneas knew that the written words of Jesus Christ are able to bring healing and deliverance so he received it by faith and was healed.

St. Matthew 8:5-13 tells the story of the Centurion's servant who was sick unto death. The Centurion sought after Jesus to heal his servant, but Jesus asked, *"Do you want me to come to your house to heal this man?*" Getting this sort of response from Jesus to some would have been interpreted as an insult, but the Centurion man understood Jesus' authority and the power of His spoken Word. He knew that the sickness had to respond and obey the command of Jesus.

He answered and said, "*Lord, speak the word only, and my servant shall be healed.*" The Word stated that his servant was healed at that very moment. According to the scriptures, we have been given the same authority. "*Thou shalt also decree and declare a thing and it shall be established unto thee.*" (Job 22:28). Also, in Acts 3:6, Peter said; "*silver and gold have I none but such as I have, I give unto you. In the name of Jesus Christ of Nazareth rise up and walk!*"

All healing is based on God's Word. If the sick receive the word of the Lord about their condition and His redemptive sacrifice for their physical and mental healing, they will not be denied. Jesus sent His Word to bring healing and deliverance; therefore, it is our duty to make it personal and receive our portion. By the wounds of Jesus you have already been healed. The Word has already been sent, and by this you are healed.

Chapter Twenty

Feeling Alone During Sickness

————◆••✳••◆————

It is very easy to feel depressed and frustrated when you are being bombarded with pain and sickness, especially in the instance when you are feeling alone. Family members may not be there, and it seems like God is not hearing or has forgotten you. I know the feeling too well, but the Word of the Lord says; "*Cast your anxiety on Him because He cares for you.*" (2 Timothy 1:7). Therefore, it is imperative to know that He cares, hears, and answers prayers.

The enemy is very cunning and strategic so in your time of sickness, he will allow you to feel neglected. Job 2-4 shows how the enemy used Job's wife and friends in his time of affliction to try and deter him from his faith in God. The enemy is cunning, so you cannot be ignorant of his devices. His desire is to isolate you so that he can have his way with you.

There is no doubt that you can feel lonely even when you are surrounded by people and you know what God's Word says about you concerning your healing. People may not fully understand what you are experiencing, but God understands your heart completely. He knows your thoughts, feels your emotion, and longs for you to know that He is with you and for you. Therefore, you must take comfort in His promises.

Promises Of God

"I will pray to the Father, and He will give you another Helper, that He may abide with you forever, the spirit of truth, I will not leave you orphans; I will come to you." (John 14:16-18).

Resist the feeling of abandonment because Jesus promises to be right there with you. He is with you through His Holy Spirit who lives in you.

"God is our refuge and strength, a very present help in trouble." (Psalm 46:1).

Many troubling situations in life can leave you feeling alone and insecure, but God is a very present help at all times.

"He heals the brokenhearted and binds up their wounds." (Psalm 147:3).

Sometimes it is a broken heart that leaves you feeling lonely, but the Lord promises to heal the wounds both physical and spiritually, and hold you close.

"In my distress I called upon the Lord, and cried out to my God; He heard my voice from His temple , and my cry came before Him, even to His ears." (Psalm 18: 6).

You never have to feel that no one hears you because your heavenly Father always hears and understands.

"For the mountains shall depart and the hills be removed, but My kindness shall not depart from you, nor shall My covenant of peace be removed; says the Lord." (Isaiah 54:10).

God is faithful; you can depend on His care and attention even if the mountains crumble around you.

Be encouraged in the Lord, for even as He is with you, so He is able and willing to heal you. Put your faith into action.

Chapter Twenty-One

The Appointed Time

Do you need a breakthrough in your health? Now is God's appointed time to heal you if you obey and follow His instructions by faith. Oftentimes people are robbed of God's intended blessings. The self-concocted idea that the old covenant promises do not apply to them is a misunderstanding of scriptures. God promises that if we are obedient and faithful, He will heal and deliver us. You have access to all the covenant promises the Lord made to His covenant people Israel through your faith in Jesus Christ. Galatians 3:9 tells us that all God's promises to Abraham are yours.

The Lord is particular about our health as He declared in His Word in 3rd John 1:2, *"Beloved I wish above all things that thou mayest prosper and be in health even as thy soul prospereth."* It is our responsibility to trust and apply His promises to our lives. We have a right to God's promises, and acknowledging this right warrants us an appointed time to access them. As you engage the healing power of God, you will not be denied.

Denial would only prove that God is not a covenant keeper; according to His Word declared in Numbers 23: 1, "*God is not a man, that he should lie; neither the son of man, that he should repent: hath he said, and shall he not do it? or hath he spoken, and shall he not make it good?*"

You may be suffering with your health for quite some time, and you may be at the point of hopelessness. There is an option; the option to believe that healing can be yours today as you read this chapter. Allow faith to rise within your heart. Pray with boldness, and believe that His infinite power is available for you. Remember, nothing is impossible for God. Don't give up! He has an appointed time for you and your miracle.

Chapter Twenty-Two

Strength In Weakness
━━━━•••❋•••━━━━

Struggling with your health can cause you become hopeless, weak, and weary, especially if you have been seeking the Lord concerning it and have seen little or no results. The Apostle Paul had a similar experience when he pleaded with God to remove his affliction, one he called a thorn in the flesh. The Lord said to Paul, "*My grace is sufficient for you, for my strength is made perfect in weakness.*" (2nd Corinthians 12:8-9). God's strength is made perfect in weakness because He delights in taking situations where human strength is lacking to demonstrate the greatness of His power.

God's denial of Paul's request for healing turned out to be a blessing. The thorn in Paul's flesh allowed him to recognize his mortality and acknowledge that he will experience weakness, despite being a powerful servant of God. The thorn also kept Paul close to the Lord. Paul's trust and confidence in God allowed him to know that He was more than able to remove the thorn in his flesh but, more so, it allowed him to recognize that God is able to give him the strength that would sustain him throughout that period in his life.

Healing is the Children's Bread

Paul stopped protesting about his situation and began to boast and take pleasure in his weakness so that the power of Christ could work through him. *"That is why for Christ sake, I delight in weaknesses, in insults, in hardships, in persecutions, in difficulties. For when I am weak, then I am strong."* (2nd Corinthians 12:10). Paul expressed the paradox of his condition that in his fragility, he was strong because his strength came from the Lord Jesus Christ.

Are you presently in a situation where you are feeling weak and helpless, whether it be physically or spiritually? God is able to give you strength, healing, and deliverance.

Over and over the Bible gives examples of God's strength manifesting when His people are weak. Moses, the great leader and prophet of Israel, was deeply aware of his human shortcomings (Exodus 4:10). When the Lord called him to go to Pharaoh, Moses cried, *"I'm not adequate, please send someone else."* But God replied, *"Go anyway, Moses, because I will be with you."* (Exodus 4:12-15).

When we find ourselves in a position of need, it allows us to see how much we need God. The more we are aware of our weakness, the more God can reveal His strength and power through us. *"We now have the light shining in our hearts, but we ourselves are like fragile clay jars containing God's great treasure."* (2nd Corinthians 4: 7). This makes it clear that our great power and strength is from God, not from ourselves.

God's strength is made perfect in weakness when we put our faith and trust in Him. The Lord's presence is all we need in times of weakness. His great power and sufficiency rest on us as we find our strength in Him, and He is glorified. We can say with the Psalmist "*My flesh and my heart may fail, but God is the strength of my heart and my portion forever.*" (Psalm 73: 26).

Chapter Twenty-Three

God's Willingness To Heal

————◦•◦❋◦•◦————

We do not fight for victory; we fight from a place of victory, resting in the finished work of Christ. Begging or pleading with God to heal us shows a lack of understanding of the ways of God and doubts in His willingness.

Oftentimes our prayers are, "God, will You please heal me," but the truth is we are asking God for something He has already done. By faith we access what is rightfully given to us by the Lord Jesus Christ. Instead, why not change the pattern of prayer? Begin to thank God according to His Word that by the stripes of Jesus we are already healed. This is a more effective way to pray, and it prevents us from doubting God's will to heal.

What does the Word say about God's willingness to heal?

In St. Luke 5:12-14, a leper came to Jesus, fell on his face, and begged Him, saying *"Lord, if you will, you can make me clean."* This scripture shows the willingness of the Lord to use His power to heal. The leper believed that Jesus could heal him but was not convinced that Jesus wanted to heal him. Is this the thought that you are struggling with? The issue is whether God is willing to release His power immediately in your body and make you whole. Jesus answered the question for those who come to him for healing in these words, "*I am willing, be clean.*"

To understand God's will concerning a specific subject, one must go to God's Word. His words are His will. The Bible tells us that healing is the will of God. The Bible also tells us, "*Forever oh Lord thy word is settled in heaven.*" (Psalm 119:89) and "*Heaven and Earth shall pass away but my (Jesus) words shall not pass away.*" (Luke 21: 33). Healing is forever a settled subject because God's Word is forever settled.

The prophet Isaiah declared God's will concerning healing when he said, "*with His stripes we are healed.*" The Apostle Peter restates God's will concerning healing in 1st Peter 2:24, "*by whose stripes ye were healed.*" Isaiah prophesied the coming of the Messiah and redemption. Peter was an eyewitness to what was described by the prophet Isaiah.

St. Matthew 8:16-17 says: "*When the even was come, they brought unto Him (Jesus) many that were possessed with devils: and He cast out the spirits with his word, and healed all that were sick. That it might be fulfilled which was spoken by Esaias (Isaiah) the prophet, saying, Himself took our infirmities and bare our sicknesses.*" (KJV – emphasis mine).

By Jesus demonstrating healing to the sick in His earthly ministry, He was fulfilling Isaiah's prophecy before He went to the cross and legally obtained redemption for us. Healing is one of the benefits of our redemption according to the Word of God. Jesus not only died and rose again for our sins, but He died and rose again for our sicknesses and diseases too. Healing belongs to us. It is part and parcel of our redemption.

Chapter Twenty-Four

Healing And Forgiveness

········✳········

ealing and forgiveness are closely connected. Being able to actively energize the act of forgiveness is very critical to receiving healing. Forgiveness is defined as a conscious decision to release negative feelings and emotions toward someone who harmed you. This does not mean you must continue to tolerate the person who harmed you but simply choose to let go of the negativity you are holding on to. Whether you are giving or receiving forgiveness, it is a very powerful thing.

"For if you forgive others (men) their trespasses, your heavenly Father will also forgive you, but if you do not forgive others their trespasses, neither will your father forgive your trespasses." (St. Matthew 6:14-15 - KJV)

Also, James 5:16 said, *"Therefore, confess your sins to one another, that you may be healed. The prayer of a righteous person has great power as it is working."*

The logos of the Lord in Exodus 15:26 says, *"if you will diligently hearken to the voice of the Lord your God, and do that which is right in his eyes, and give ear to his commandments and keep all his statues, I will put none of the diseases on you that I put on the Egyptians, for I am the Lord, your healer."*

Forgiveness is very critical to one's health and wellbeing. Forgiving yourself and others will allow you to heal in all areas of your life: mentally, physically, emotionally, and spiritually. Learning to forgive has benefits that are far greater than we may think.

Grudges are like toxins within our emotions. When you learn to eliminate these toxins, your body begins to heal and returns to homeostasis (its natural state of balance). Forgiving and healing are gifts we give to ourselves in the form of internal peace and stability. From the moment you begin the process of forgiving, your body starts healing. Forgiveness automatically triggers healing.

Forgiveness can lead to higher self-esteem. It allows you to have a greater spiritual connection through which the miraculous act of healing can take place.

"Jesus seeing their faith said to the paralytic, son, your sins are forgiven. But some of the scribes were reasoning in their hearts who can forgive sins but God alone? He said to the paralytic, I say to you, get up, pick up your pallet and go home." (St. Mark 2:5-11).

Here, Jesus was demonstrating that there is a connection between the physical and emotional parts of our lives. In fact, it is said today by doctors that there is a strong link between forgiveness and health. There are three lessons from this story.

1. Jesus can heal any disease and solve any problem.
2. He is concerned about your whole being; not just your body, but your thoughts and emotions.
3. There is a connection between health and forgiveness.

Remember, *"if we confess our sins, He is faithful and righteous to forgive us our sins and cleanse us from all unrighteousness" (1 John 1:9).* Accept His forgiveness and be the messenger of forgiveness in the life of others. Let Him wash away your guilt and heal you.

Chapter Twenty-Five

Faith Healing

━━━╸•◦❋◦•╺━━━

What Is Faith?

"Without faith no one can please God. Anyone who comes to God must believe that He is real and that He rewards those who diligently seek Him." (Hebrews 11:6).

Faith means belief, firm persuasion, assurance, firm conviction, and faithfulness. Faith is confidence in what we hope for and the assurance that the Lord is working, even though we cannot see it. Faith knows that no matter what the situation in our lives or someone else's, the Lord is working on it.

It is the act whereby a person lays hold of God's resources, becomes obedient to what He has prescribed and, putting aside all self interest and self-reliance, trusts Him completely. It is an unqualified surrender of the whole of one's being in dependence upon Him. It is wholly trusting and relying upon Him for all things. It is not just mental assent to the facts and realities of truth; it must come from a deep inner conviction. St. James 2:19 tells us that the demons also believe.

Healing is the Children's Bread

"Trust in the Lord with all your heart and lean not to your own understanding." (Proverbs 3:5).

"He that trusts in his own heart is a fool but whoso walketh wisely, he shall be delivered." (Proverbs 28:26).

Faith will compel us to invite God into our lives and maintain a relationship with Him through prayer. We should pray every day and throughout the day. It is impossible to pray too much. We can pray for protection, forgiveness, guidance, understanding, and peace. We can express our love, gratitude, needs, worries, and fears. We should pray boldly and be generous with our prayers for others. Trust that God will hear your prayers and respond. Listen and watch for ways that God may be speaking to you. They may not be in the form and the timeframe that you are expecting. And when your prayers are answered, remember to give thanks to God. Without prayer, we are strangers to God.

Faith encourages us to place God in the center and forefront of our lives. We should not allow the situations and circumstances of our lives to distract us from living a life that honours God.

When you are going through a difficult time, be it emotional, physical, mental, or spiritual, it can be easy to lose faith. Some challenges in life can make you feel like you may not overcome them or the pain is almost too much to bear. However, the good news is that you can move past these moments, sometimes simply by knowing that the Lord does not throw anything your way that you cannot handle and that He is with you regardless of how you are feeling and that He will help you to endure difficult and trying times. The Word of the Lord concerning healing will inspire and allow you to embrace healing in a way that helps you grow, even through the tough times.

Scriptures:

James 5:15
And the prayer offered in faith will restore the one who is sick, and the Lord will raise him up, and if he has committed sins, they will be forgiven him.

James 5:14
Is anyone among you sick? Then he must call for the elders of the church and they are to pray over him, anointing him with oil in the name of the Lord;

Mark 10:52
And Jesus said to him, "Go; your faith has made you well." Immediately he regained his sight and began following Him on the road.

Matthew 15:28
Then Jesus said to her, "O woman, your faith is great; it shall be done for you as you wish." And her daughter was healed at once.

Jeremiah 17:14

Healing is the Children's Bread

Heal me, O Lord, and I will be healed; save me and I will be saved, for You are my praise.

Chapter Twenty-Six

The Gift Of Healing

In 1 Corinthians 12:7-11, Paul lists several gifts of the Holy Spirit, including the gift of healing. Paul did not want the church in Corinth to be uninformed.

"Now to each one the manifestation of the Spirit is given for the common good. To one there is given through the Spirit a message of wisdom, to another a message of knowledge by means of the same Spirit, to another faith by the same Spirit, to another the gifts of healing by that same Spirit…"

The gift of healing is different from the healing most of us experience through the common grace of medical intervention. The gift of healing is when the Holy Spirit heals someone from a disease or infirmity supernaturally.

We see this in the gospels and the book of Acts, when Jesus' disciples healed people through prayer, anointing with oil, or the power of their words.

- Peter and John told a lame beggar outside the temple to get up and walk, and he did (see Acts 3:1-10).
- Philip preached the gospel in Samaria and healed many who were paralyzed or lame (see Acts 8:4-8).
- Peter told a paralyzed man named Aeneas to get out of bed and walk, and he did (see Acts 9:32-35). Peter also prayed for a woman named Dorcas, and she came back to life (see Acts 9:36-43).

The same Holy Spirit who worked through Peter, John, Paul, and all of the disciples lives in us. If God chose to supernaturally heal people back then, why wouldn't He do the same today? According to the scripture, He is the same yesterday, today, and forever. He has not changed. His work and word remain the same, and it is therefore critical that we believe them.

In Mark's account of the great commission, Jesus stated that one of the signs to follow believers in Him would be healing after the laying on of hands. In the epistle of James chapter five, anointing with oil is involved with the laying on of hands and prayer over the sick. These symbolise that believers were channels of divine power and that healing is the work of the Holy Spirit. Healing is also connected with the forgiveness of sins.

All Believers are encouraged to pray for the healing of the sick even if they do not claim possession of the supernatural gift. The gift of healing is not for self-exaltation but for the sake of love.

Gifts of healings and workings of miracles could easily become the basis of pride, just like teaching, preaching, mercy, hospitality, prophecy, or any other gifts, but they are meant to be expressions of love. Paul says in 1 Corinthians 13:2, *"Though I have all faith so as to remove mountains, but have not love, I am nothing."* Gifts are not the main thing. Love is the main thing, and using gifts is one way to love.

This is what Paul says in 1 Corinthians 12:7, *"To each is given the manifestation of the Spirit for the common good."* It is a great danger to want signs and wonders because they sound good, seem exciting, or merely because you think they would make your faith stronger. That is almost a sure way to spiritual self-centeredness. Instead, we should strive to honour Christ through our self-sacrificing love for others. The greatest need we have is not for gifts of healing but rather to demonstrate compassion for people who are sick with soul-destroying sin, emotional disorders, physical disease, and, in some cases, a mix of all three. The greatest miracle is when our hearts begin to care more about the loss and pain of others than about our own personal comforts and gain. When that miracle happens, we might be in a position to experience the gift of healing.

In conclusion, the gift of healing is:

1. **All for the sake of love.**

The gifts should be for the sake of love. So, let the love of Jesus break us down and build us up to love others.

2. Not the ability to heal at will.

If God gives you gifts of healing, it does not mean you can heal at will or that everyone you pray for will be healed. God gave the apostle Paul the grace to heal the crippled man in Lystra (see Acts 14:10), many people in Ephesus (see Acts 19:12), the demonized girl in Philippi (see Acts 16:18), and Eutychus when he was taken up dead after falling out of a window (see Acts 20:9–10). But Paul could not heal himself from the thorn in the flesh (see 2 Corinthians 12:8–9) or from the ailment that he had when he preached in Galatia (see Galatians 4:13–14). Evidently, he could not heal Timothy from his stomach ailments (see 1 Timothy 5:23) or Epaphroditus from his life-threatening sickness (see Philippians 2:26–27) or Trophimus whom he "left ill at Miletus" (see 2 Timothy 4:20). Sometimes Paul was given the gift of healing and sometimes he was not. God is sovereign in this affair. Nothing is mechanical or automatic.

So the wording of 1 Corinthians 12:9, as well as Paul's own experience, teaches us that there are varied gifts of healings that can be given to us at different times for different illnesses. However, there are no guarantees that because we have received a gift to heal in the past, we will receive one in any specific case in the future. Verse 11 says it is the Spirit who "apportions the gifts to each one individually as he pleases." He is sovereign and can give or withhold a gift of healing whenever it pleases Him.

3. Rightly to be sought.

This suggests that we may rightly seek for gifts of healing which is implied in the pursuit of love and compassion. Praying for healing is only one way to show love to someone. Once we realize this, we may be led to seek the gifts. According to 1st Corinthians 14:1. *"Make love your aim, and earnestly desire the spiritual gifts."*

Setting your heart on the pursuit of love will position you to be zealous for spiritual gifts. Among those spiritual gifts are *"gifts of healings."* Therefore, I think 1st Corinthians 14:1 implores us to seek this gift. It is subordinate to love, and it is not among the greater gifts like prophecy, but it is one of the humble lesser gifts of God. We would do well not to reject, despise or exaggerate it. We should simply seek with all our hearts to do good to each other and pray humbly that, if God permits, you would be granted gifts of healing for the blessing of the church, God's people, and the glory of His name in the earth.

Chapter Twenty-Seven

Healing From Barrenness

I can remember in the year 2020, a young lady reached out to me for prayer. She was in desperate need of a child. This young woman had been married for a few years. She tried numerous times to become pregnant but to no avail. She went to doctors who told her she was not capable of having children because of a condition she suffered from.

However, she believed that the Lord was able to change her story, so we agreed in prayer. I prayed the prayer of faith and healing over her and declared the Word of the Lord. A few months later, she messaged me with the good news. She was pregnant and was happily waiting for her delivery. God still heals from barrenness.

The story of Elkanah and Hannah is another beautiful reminder that God will remember us in our struggles. In Samuel 1:9-19, Hannah implored the Lord to bless her with a child, promising that she would give him to the Lord all the days of his life. The Lord remembered Hannah in her infertility and blessed her with Samuel.

The profound words *"and the Lord remembered her"* (Samuel 1:19), are a healing reminder that even in our doubts and insecurities about the Lord, He remembers us, carries us through hardships, and will bless our lives abundantly. He understands the struggle with infertility and our desire to be filled with life. Though the Lord's timing is unknown, the story of Hannah's conception of Samuel reminds us that He will remember us. He will heal us emotionally, spiritually, and physically.

"Is anything too hard for the Lord to do?" (Genesis 18:14)

Abraham and Sarah's journey through infertility highlights the importance of radical trust in the Lord's plan. Constantly throughout scripture, Abraham puts his faith in the Lord and honours His requests.

When Sarah learned that she and Abraham would bear a child in their old age, Sarah laughed. God spoke to Abraham, *"Why did Sarah laugh and say, 'will I really bear a child, old as I am?' Is anything too hard for the Lord to do?"* (Genesis 18:13-14). Sarah was slow to believe that God would love her enough to send her the marvelous gift of a child.

We may doubt God's plan for our lives, but He calls us to trust Him radically. His faithfulness is enduring, and His plan is marvelous. Sarah was healed from infertility in her old age and blessed with a child, Isaac. Are you suffering from barrenness/infertility? God is able to perform the same miracle in your life.

God Hears And Answers Our Prayers

The remarkable conception of Samson by Manoah and his wife affirms that the Lord works wonders and hears our prayers. The Lord sent an angel to Manoah's wife to tell her that she would bear a son, Samson. In Manoah's disbelief, he prayed to the Lord that He might send the angel again. *"God heard the prayer of Manoah"* and sent the angel once more (see Judges 13:9).

Manoah and his wife's disbelief and humility in the healing of their infertility beautifully encourages us to remember that the Lord does hear our prayers. The story of Samson's conception can revive our faith that God is working all things out for our good. He is our Creator, Supplier, Master, Healer, and Provider. He continues to be faithful. Will You trust Him today?

Chapter Twenty-Eight

Healing From Emotional Hurt

"He heals the brokenhearted and binds up their wounds."
(Psalm 147:3).

Emotional healing is something that every person needs, to one degree or another. We have all been wounded emotionally. Emotional brokenness and pain vary between people as everyone is different. Whether the cause is natural or because of another's sin, the majority of people fight some type of emotional battle. Some of the most common symptoms of emotional harm are sleeplessness, detachment, depression, anger, isolation, bitterness, frustration, and fear.

The ordeal of experiencing emotional hurt is catastrophic and has the ability to also destroy a person's ego and self-esteem. I have gone through emotional hurt, and as such, I am able to share how I have been healed through the power of the Holy Spirit and the Word of God. Some time ago, I was rejected, belittled, and talked down to by someone who I believed the Lord placed in my life as a role model and destiny helper. I tried to be obedient to the instructions I received from the Lord so I was committed and determined to pursue and move forward into purpose and destiny.

However, in the midst of doing all of that, the enemy was not pleased so he tried to find a way to abort the purpose of the Lord in my life. I became weak and vulnerable, but then I remembered who I am and that my God is faithful. He is able to deliver. I was confident in His Word that He who hath begun a good work is able to complete it until the day of Jesus Christ (see Philippians 1:6).

The pain and hurt were real, but all things will work together for the good of those who love God and are called according to His purpose (see Romans 8:28). In my season of turmoil and distress, I was reminded by a prophet of the Lord that "destiny can be delayed but it certainly cannot be denied." It's amazing how God is on time and knows just when to send help through the medium He chooses. I have been bruised and scarred, but God's power to heal the brokenhearted is still available. Are you hurting and need emotional healing at this moment? As you read this chapter, may you receive healing in Jesus' name.

Here are some biblical truths about receiving your healing today.

- Meditate on God's Word, the Bible. God's instructions are "life to those who find them and health to one's whole body" (Proverbs 4:22). The person "whose delight is in the law of the Lord, and who meditates on his law day and night" is blessed (Psalm 1:1-2).

- Confess any known sin to God. Then take God at His word: "If we confess our sins, he is faithful and just and will forgive us our sins and purify us from all unrighteousness" (1 John 1:9).

- Take control of your thoughts by allowing the Holy Spirit to take control of those thoughts. In the Spirit, "we take captive every thought to make it obedient to Christ" (2 Corinthians 10:5).

- Refuse to fall back into old, sinful habits. "We know that our old self was crucified with him so that the body ruled by sin might be done away with, that we should no longer be slaves to sin" (Romans 6:6). You have been called to holiness and to walk in the newness of life (see Romans 6:4).

- Forgive those who have hurt you. This is important. "Be kind and compassionate to one another, forgiving each other, just as in Christ God forgave you" (see Ephesians 4:32). Be cautious of any root of bitterness in the soul (see Hebrews 12:15).

- See yourself as God sees you: loved (see Romans 5:8); gifted (see 2 Timothy 1:7); set free (see John 8:36); and washed, sanctified, and justified (see 1 Corinthians 6:11).

- Get involved in a Bible-teaching local church and open yourself to their fellowship and teaching ministry. God gives spiritual gifts to His church "to equip his people for works of service, so that the body of Christ may be built up" (Ephesians 4:12). Part of a church's function is to aid the healing process of those who are emotionally or spiritually wounded.

- We are able to receive healing from emotional hurt through Jesus Christ; His Spirit is a Spirit of kindness, selflessness, truth, and trustworthiness, and He finds joy in producing such qualities in us (see Galatians 5:22-23; 1 John 3:19-24). When we are indwelt with His Spirit, He can and will delight to turn us around and make us the kind of people who can trust and be trusted by others, resulting in better relationships all around (see John 7:38).

Chapter Twenty-Nine

Healing Is The Children's Bread

———————•◦❋◦•———————

"Healing is the children's bread." These are the words I heard in my spirit while I was feeling very ill in September 2020. I laid in bed feeling so helpless and enduring much pain. The thought of asking someone to pray for me came to my mind several times, but I did not make an attempt. Finally, the Spirit of the Lord began to minister to me. "The word is in you; declare it out of your mouth." As I heard these words, I began to declare it over my body. After uttering in faith; "healing is the children's bread" several times, the Spirit of the Lord continued to minister to me both spiritually and physically. How do I know that the promise from the Lord is true? I have not only read it in the scriptures, but I have personally experienced it. As a result of my experience of God's healing power, this book was birthed.

In St. Mark 7:27: Jesus said unto her, *"let the children first be filled; for it is not meet to take the children" bread and cast it unto the dogs."* Here Jesus was speaking to a Gentile woman who came to Jesus because her child was sick and needed healing. Jesus told her that the bread he had (healing) was for the children (the Jews).

The gospel was not yet extended to the Gentile world in that time, but the woman did not take offense to the response from Jesus; she understood what He carried and replied that even the crumbs that fell from the master's table belonged to the dogs. Jesus was touched by the woman's response and immediately, her child received healing. The disposition of her heart and the level of her faith were what really spoke to Jesus. What is the position of your heart and faith in regards to the promises of the Lord? Thank God that in Christ Jesus today, we all have access to the blessings, promises, and covenants that God promised to the nation of Israel.

The important implication for us today is that Jesus indirectly called healing the children's bread. Bread in a home is a child's privilege, and it is the father's responsibility to ensure it is provided for his child. Jesus spoke in Matthew 7:11, *"If ye then, being evil know how to give good gifts unto your children, how much more shall your Father which is in heaven give good things to them that ask?"*

One way that Jesus has made provision for His children is through healing and deliverance; once you are in God's family, you are entitled to it. He has provided the bread, and it is our responsibility to eat that bread until we are filled. The Lord wants you to be healed and delivered from all infirmities and under every circumstance. Be confident in His provision. Meditate, apply the Word, and pray and you shall receive your portion of healing.

Chapter Thirty

Prayer For Healing

—◆•◆❋◆•◆—

My sovereign King and Creator, the One who rules in the affairs of men; Jehovah Rapha, You are worthy, You are amazing and faithful. You are the God that is a covenant keeper, and for that, I give You thanks. I worship and reverence You, Abba.

Your words declare that at the mention of Your name every knee shall bow, and every tongue shall confess that Jesus Christ is Lord to the glory of God. Lord, I bless You because Your Word declare that healing is the children's bread. You were wounded for our transgressions; You were bruised for our iniquities; the chastisement of our peace was upon You, and by Your stripes, we are healed.

Lord, You said that You will heal me, and I shall be healed. Today, I stand on the authority of Your Word and declare that You are a healer, the greatest physician, the balm in Gilead and I speak the word of healing over my mind, emotions and body. Father, Your Word declare that my body is the temple of the Holy Spirit and where the Spirit of the Lord lives, there no infirmities will dwell. I take authority and ask that You elevate my faith in this hour as I receive Your healing touch in Jesus' name. I break the backbone of the spirit of infirmity over my life, and I declare that I am healed, in Jesus' name. Amen!

About The Author

Deneise Fearon is a mother, wife, prophetic minister (apostle elect), an amazon best-selling and award-winning author, speaker, and Christian life coach. Having endured many life changes and faith-testing trials, and driven by her genuine love for people, she uses her experiences and the Word of God to empower the body of Christ to live victorious lives. Through her coaching program, she helps individuals who are feeling stuck or stagnant in their growth, spiritual walk, and faith to discover their passion so they can fulfill their God-given purpose.

www.ingramcontent.com/pod-product-compliance
Lightning Source LLC
Chambersburg PA
CBHW071953110426
42744CB00030B/1231